THESE STREETS

Published by Goldfish Press
4545 42nd Avenue Southwest
Suite 211
Seattle, Washington, 98116

Manufactured in the United States of America

ISBN 13: 978-1-950276-04-2
ISBN 10: 1-950276-04-x

Library of Congress Catalog Card Number 2019912919

Cover design by J. Edward Moss
Photos by the authors
Book design by Susan Steiner

This book was set on the Monotype Arial

THESE STREETS

**Poems by
J. Edward Moss
&
John Burgess**

**Goldfish Press
Seattle**

INTRODUCTION

The Symbiosis of Cities

Jazz great Bill Evans seems the antithesis to the rush and grit of living in a city. It's as if time and motion for him were dialed back, projected in slow-mo so you can witness each blur, each passing moment, clearly and wide-eyed.
    "to slow it down…"

Cities stand at collision points. Where geography and history, where native cultures and pioneer righteousness, where commerce and livelihood, run/ran head-on into each other. The wreckage can be disorientating.

Experienced from inside bars, cities eventually become dark and grungy. The lounge pianist hitting chords and keys that alternately mimic/mock what's happening outside on these streets. We end up living in our own heads.
    "congruent with the city / and losing its context"

When you choose to live in a city you choose improvisation, you choose collaboration. Communal and commiserate are common concerns. You react to what the other player lays down ahead of you, an action and reaction, a call and a response.
    "i sway when you sway"

My nephew J. Edward Moss camped along the Genesee River in Rochester, N.Y., near the shores of great Lake Ontario. And I ensconced in the fort at Seattle, Wash., on the shores of Puget Sound. We are two poets from different cities riffing on shared titles. Responding to each other's lines with lines that complement and collide, intertwine like jazz musicians or stumble home like drunken Beats.

Stopping the rush for a moment to see what's left.   —*jb*

THESE STREETS

Note: These poems were composed, edited and/or arranged while listening to recordings of jazz pianist Bill Evans

.

THESE STREETS GREET ANOTHER YEAR

(Rochester)

lost in paper cups
        how distinct your years are.

could reach me at any moment remembering
        every wrinkle.

they're somewhat like distant offspring
        i fathered for stability.

there is no stability in selfishness
        as we come to know.

there are no polished platinum streets,
        just confetti covering us.

we turn clockwise toward a door
        neck cocked to the side

barely awake enough to see
        what comes after.

THESE STREETS GREET ANOTHER YEAR

(Seattle)

call it my fucked-up year
the year nothing made sense
nothing i said mattered
it was all the wrong tense—

that year the city repaved
ignored strolling on aurora
bulldozed those encampments

pots & pans banging
you & i witnessed fireworks
middle of the street.

THESE STREETS FOLLOW ME HOME

(Seattle)

pissing where
this city reaches
its limits

shortest distance
between bar
& home is

missing
sidewalks
uneven &
unmapped.

THESE STREETS FOLLOW ME HOME

(Rochester)

and so evening finds
sound of closing
time in a week
night, uneventful.

getting home long after
most have hushed their heads.

streets sounding off
their sour mantra...

"trace us once
you've traced us always."

THESE STREETS ARE BATHED IN SHADOW

(Rochester)

yes, i'll admit
i ate the sun raw
no sugar
        no salt no pepper

no rise no set
        just as is
                where it sat
amongst the cosmos.

sure our planet suffered
but, i was fed up.
        shiny bastard always startin' a fuss
so damn early each day.

so yes,
        darkness all the time
        was a choice
                i had to make
in the night
        i am level
        and clear
in the night
        i am without
        nudity
        i am cloaked
        with clarity

so i chose to keep us all in the dark.

THESE STREETS ARE BATHED IN SHADOW

(Seattle)

we spend our days under cover
of gray like wet cement
leaves us in a druggy fog
where matters aren't that set

wrapped in strips of musty linen
there's no distinction here
no discerning sky from street no
telling if things have ended

we stumble thru nothingness
our view of heaven hidden.

THESE STREETS ARE DEAD QUIET

(Rochester)

on the porch
smoke dissipates to a memory blowing
away from town.

too busy to disturb this twilight.
moon stumbles by.

patches of catastrophe hang out their windows.
music is nowhere...

no headlights to paint dark
they are off drifting in tiny orbits.

stuffed between families and loners
and lonely couples
a band of misfit losers wanders on.

out of steps.
full of worries.
chewed them up.
spit them sideways.

in the shadows and shade
they raise such hell.
soft notes
dog snores.
drag pulls
and wallets on empty.

this is all they have
when the noise catches up.

THESE STREETS ARE DEAD QUIET

(Seattle)

2 a.m. amplifies
what's not there

new moon
presses down like
atmosphere

you cover your ears for
fear of loneliness

you won't hear
the opening window
nor her caress.

THESE STREETS ARE AWAKENED

(Rochester)

with each passing day
time clashes and elapses
evaporates and dances
stupefied...enchanted.

it's what some call a passage.

if you concentrate
you can't miss how
days fall to unwatered messes.
soft and soiled chances
broken chandeliers in foreign mansions.

it is nothing we accept yet,
only know the stances.
commonly repeated stanzas in the form
of anthem gospels blasted.
to slow it down…
as sunlight fills each mattress.

THESE STREETS ARE AWAKENED

(Seattle)

my eyes wrapped
in limited visibility

shrouded thinned
to splitting edge

moment when
cutting first cuts

illumination erases
night like a mistake

blindness & blinds
slowly rise.

THESE STREETS REPEAT MY NAME

(Rochester)

looking out at a weary square
this side of not quite paradise
but, belonging.

--there...amongst fading red
brake lights are dreams
balancing in my vision.

streets, cracked faces,
rounded edges...

i hold them all,
and nothing seems intangible.

THESE STREETS REPEAT MY NAME

(Seattle)

i hear my name
in passing traffic
in rushing to be
somewhere
not clear
who in muffled
tone
alone
finds volume

again i hear my name.

THESE STREETS FEED A METROPOLITAN SCENE (IN THE KEY OF A-MINOR)

(Rochester)

this is a proper tone to lob obscenities at
        a tone-deaf town
chasing side streets with a staccato-like importance
toward a desperate crescendo
as waves of symphonic madness drown to
        a metronome's nagging.

this score seems ruthless if not survived
        or at least sight-read.

it unfurls any time or place and
        you must mind your notes

                eye your accents

                    land your solos.

THESE STREETS FEED A METROPOLITAN SCENE (IN THE KEY OF A-MINOR)

(Seattle)

rolling weight of tremolo time
like waves eroding city walls

what sound is left
after pit is dug

how at first light lone crow
com-PLAINS-com-PLAINS

the way bass riff rumbles
& wedges near your heart

or regrade traffic keeps going
fuck-slappp-fuck-slappp-fuck-slappp.

THESE STREETS FROM 6 TO 6 TO 6

(Rochester)

come rain, or shine
flowers dine amongst our feet
rising from where cigarette butts
play hide 'n' seek.

come rain, come drought each tune sits
on backyard fences waiting for mischief.

come sun or hurricane playing for keeps
wild ones make bets in basements.

come whispers come shouts
ice melts
leaving pools for a neighborhood of dreamers
bettering comfortable clouds.

heading in for the daily grind.

THESE STREETS FROM 6 TO 6 TO 6

(Seattle)

attics are a luxury
they're what i imagine
the other side to be

a crow
walks on the roof
i can hear her
crossing

flat on my back
i dream of
clouds.

ENOUGH WITH THESE STREETS

(Rochester)

unsettled by patterns
heading down a homeward path.

one of four ways
to arrive safely
before my dying apartment block.

same cast of characters
scattered up and down
i nod to them
but, my head weighs a ton

and soon the season changes
but, i have only just begun
to lift my eyes.

ENOUGH WITH THESE STREETS

(Seattle)

crows congregate
rage against
november wind

barricaded streets
detour traffic
in misdirected rush

as our time expires
other passengers blur
in streaks of rain

we arrive too late.

THESE STREETS ARE USELESS

(Rochester)

these streets don't mock   me
same as they used   to.

they sure don't off   er
comfort   --never have.

staring at me   like
children ready for learning.

warm & dark those chalkboard side   walks
chase urgency to fill the board.

THESE STREETS ARE USELESS

(Seattle)

O sweet jesus
wasted & lonely
stumbling home

if i repent
late in life
let it be
broken & bruised

spinning like
hank williams
on a 45.

THESE STREETS ARE WET AFTER IT RAINS

(Seattle)

how do we measure
what accumulates
& what we piss away

count the river tap-
tap-tapping on our
shuttered window or

long for what's gone
drained by development

music plays from some
where down the block.

THESE STREETS ARE WET AFTER IT RAINS

(Rochester)

bill evans sounds from my stereo.

"like tears in the rain"

i remember a time
where all i noticed
was the weather
whether it mattered at all.

(HOW) THESE STREETS CARRY ON

(Seattle)

battle or be embattled
be ready for a beating
become bewildered by
what matters most
better not bash
better not boast
be beholden to being
better than before
behind barricades
battered & bunkered.

(HOW) THESE STREETS CARRY ON

(Rochester)

broken and buffered
completely content to
cope with complex comments
on concrete vomit
art on sides of community center complex
and convents say,
"COMMUNICATE OR CONFESS"
caught commotion in cobwebs
congruent with the city
and losing its context.

THESE STREETS (& OTHER THINGS)
FALL APART

(Seattle)

waves work overtime
to get the shore to let go

sea-soaked pilings prop up
planks rotting inside out

hearts & tunneling machines
leave sinkholes in their wake

concrete
falls
from
overhead.

THESE STREETS (& OTHER THINGS)
FALL APART

(Rochester)

flags never fixed.
ripped,
becoming untethered.

faded billboards
mumble quietly
huddled together.

trees replaced
with NEW APARTMENT HOUSING
eating what was left.

the wear
& tear
of everyday abuse.

THESE STREETS ACT ALL INDIGNANT

(Seattle)

O dear barfly

how bubbles
rise in your
glass burst
at the surface

how your piss
rivers into alleys

how we
become
one.

THESE STREETS ACT ALL INDIGNANT

(Rochester)

chasing what seems to be
an endless bottom.
more glasses fall
--break lipstick stains in two.

barkeep,
(need not ask)
simply pours.

spun 'round this hole.
these same faces
set in stone.

THESE STREETS: KITTY-CORNER
TO THE DRUG HOUSE

(Rochester)

pull up   get out
engine on   dogs yapping

tap tap   tapping door
ring bell   keys lost

phone's dead   head's gone
brain's full   always fed

all hours   every hour
tap tapping   time out

horn blares   too high
too often   sub woofs

trap kicks   trap rhymes
trapped outside   doorstep frenzy

ring bell   bell rung
head spun   fire eyed

kickflip disrespect   night's on
bang bang   shattered fist

any more?   honk honk
how the   hell do

they keep this up?

THESE STREETS: KITTY-CORNER
TO THE DRUG HOUSE

(Seattle)

rats left first
followed by the squatters
a bulldozer took down in hours
what years of complaints
couldn't make come clean

candles extinguished
the hole was filled
traffic eventually calmed

& the couple who built there
divorced soon after moving in.

HOW MUCH THESE STREETS COST

(Rochester)

up to my ne
ck in bill
s

they don't stop.

like buffalo once roamed
far n wide
now, piled on my doorstep.

life
less, still so he
                    avy.

HOW MUCH THESE STREETS COST

(Seattle)

lit
the way
is paved
wired &
curbed

over bones
broken tools
settlements
& fires
sit.

THESE STREETS LEAVE ME BRUISED
& BLEEDING

(Rochester)

if a hand bleeds then all falls down and apart.

if eyes are keys to the soul
then hands are the lock.

before you know it i won't do anything
              --PARALYSIS WILL HAVE ME.

each move i'll hesitate and say,
"look at these hands...who could i lend them to?"

you too will stare down seeing your dents/bruises/
              bleeding/peeling too
and you'll ask yourself the same.

until,
there we are
in a room with no eyes
our hands
covered by miles of bandages
looking for a pair of scissors.

THESE STREETS LEAVE ME BRUISED
& BLEEDING

(Seattle) (for J.W.)

when you fall nothing
stops you—

not air
not hands
not sirens

—your skull gives way
to anarchies

a rush then
blankness
then concrete.

THESE STREETS HOW THEY OVERFLOW

(Rochester)

perverts
purveyors
       and prayers
players and
      the played
      the plagued
      play of trudging
            on
the down 'n' out
      killers with the diamond mouths.
the pride riding faceless
shadows across a bar,
      this bar, this evening
inside this bubble blown
these smiles are coiled
these rules and laws like ropes
tightened and tightening still.

this sure is the city
full of grace and ill will.

THESE STREETS HOW THEY OVERFLOW

(Seattle)

with what's left of
last night's desire—

an angel
outlined
in piss

a big gulp
spilled
like vomit

a single stiletto
kicked aside.

HIGH ABOVE THESE STREETS

(Rochester)

sunshine hits iris
first time in 8 days.
warming bone against bone
tone of a day off.

off the meds
cold turkey
ain't never settled so smoothly.

what once was tame
was a straight line.

back to peaks and valleys again.

watching ants
assembling below.

HIGH ABOVE THESE STREETS

(Seattle)

curves & waves
give way to straight

leave triangles
in their wake

lines confuse
what's true north

i see how
geometry shapes
the way i go

i sway when you sway

ABOUT THE AUTHORS

J. Edward Moss is a Rochester, N.Y., based poet as of 2015. He has self-published two books and currently resides in the heart of the city -- making music and operating as an entrepreneur in social media and graphic design.

John Burgess has lived and worked in Seattle since 1985. He is co-instigator with the Band of Poets, a collaboration between poets and musicians. He has written five books of poetry, including *Punk Poems*.

www.ingramcontent.com/pod-product-compliance
Lightning Source LLC
Chambersburg PA
CBHW021940170626
46807CB00007B/3212